You have the ability to
create the future you want.

Take your thoughts
and create goals.

CREATE YOUR SUCCESS.

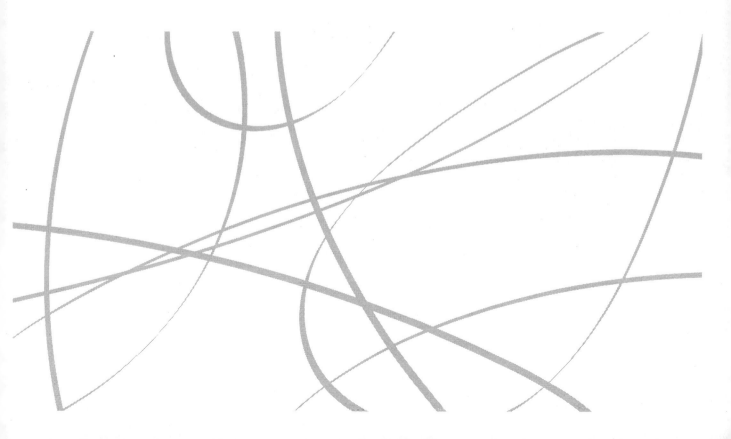

INSTRUCTIONS

1. Review the entire planner before you get started.

2. Complete all the areas of the planner that you can now.

3. Complete your academic and personal goals.

4. Review your goals weekly, and make adjustments as required. Visualize yourself achieving your goals. You have to believe it to achieve it. Mark of in the weekly goal assessment that you have reviewed your goals.

5. Complete the areas of your planner that are specific to your academic year as needed.

6. Create and follow your weekly schedule each week. Prioritize your tasks. Wake up with energy and clarity to work towards achieving your goals.

7. Daily actions are your homework and any practices you have. Having a plan helps you move toward achieving your goals and it creates personal accountability and personal responsibility. You are the author of your story, create it.

WEEKLY REFLECTIONS

End each with your reflections, wins and what you want to take away with you for the week to come. This weekly practice will excel your growth and success.

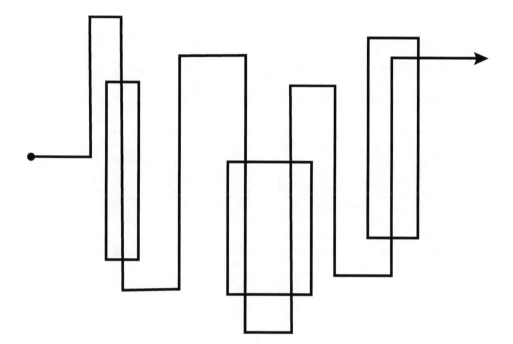

LET'S
DO THIS

20 ___ SCHOOL YEAR
COMPLETE WITH SCHOOL HOLIDAYS, EXAMS AND EVENTS.

	SUNDAY	MONDAY	TUESDAY	WEDNESDAY	THURSDAY	FRIDAY	SATURDAY
JULY							
AUGUST							
SEPTEMBER							
OCTOBER							
NOVEMBER							
DECEMBER							

	SUNDAY	MONDAY	TUESDAY	WEDNESDAY	THURSDAY	FRIDAY	SATURDAY
JANUARY							
FEBRUARY							
MARCH							
APRIL							
MAY							
JUNE							

MY SCHEDULE

COMPLETE WITH SCHOOL HOLIDAYS, EXAMS AND EVENTS.

MY SCHEDULE

COMPLETE WITH SCHOOL HOLIDAYS, EXAMS AND EVENTS.

MY SCHEDULE
COMPLETE WITH SCHOOL HOLIDAYS, EXAMS AND EVENTS.

MY SCHEDULE
COMPLETE WITH SCHOOL HOLIDAYS, EXAMS AND EVENTS.

MY SCHEDULE

COMPLETE WITH SCHOOL HOLIDAYS, EXAMS AND EVENTS.

MY SCHEDULE

COMPLETE WITH SCHOOL HOLIDAYS, EXAMS AND EVENTS.

MY SCHEDULE

COMPLETE WITH SCHOOL HOLIDAYS, EXAMS AND EVENTS.

MY SCHEDULE

COMPLETE WITH SCHOOL HOLIDAYS, EXAMS AND EVENTS.

GOALS

A goal is your call to action, it is what I am going to do and how am I going to do it. By being clear about what you want and how you are going to get it you write a goal, your dream becomes a reality and you create your motivation to achieve your goals. Here you will write your S.M.A.R.T. GOALS. Create academic, extracurricular and personal goals.

GOAL

_____

_____

_____

_____

_____

_____

OBJECTIVES

Objectives are the steps to achieve your goals. Creating accountability and responsibility for creating your pathway to success. An objective may be, To do all the homework and turn it in on time.

OBJECTIVE/
DEFINITION

_____

_____

_____

_____

_____

_____

WEEKLY ASSESSMENT

We were going to put in how to use it. Here check off each week that you have read your goal and you are working at achieving it. Or celebrate that you have achieved it.

WEEKLY ASSESSMENT OF GOAL

01	02	03	04	05	06	07	08	09	10	11	12	13	14	15	16	17	18	19	20	21	22	23	24	25	26
27	28	29	30	31	32	33	34	35	36	37	38	39	40	41	42	43	44	45	46	47	48	49	50	51	52

GOAL

_____

_____

_____

_____

_____

OBJECTIVES

_____

_____

_____

_____

_____

_____

_____

_____

_____

_____

WEEKLY ASSESSMENT OF GOAL

01	02	03	04	05	06	07	08	09	10	11	12	13	14	15	16	17	18	19	20	21	22	23	24	25	26
27	28	29	30	31	32	33	34	35	36	37	38	39	40	41	42	43	44	45	46	47	48	49	50	51	52

GOAL

_____

_____

_____

_____

_____

OBJECTIVES

_____

_____

_____

_____

_____

_____

_____

_____

_____

WEEKLY ASSESSMENT OF GOAL

01	02	03	04	05	06	07	08	09	10	11	12	13	14	15	16	17	18	19	20	21	22	23	24	25	26
27	28	29	30	31	32	33	34	35	36	37	38	39	40	41	42	43	44	45	46	47	48	49	50	51	52

GOAL

_____

_____

_____

_____

_____

OBJECTIVES

_____

_____

_____

_____

_____

_____

_____

_____

_____

WEEKLY ASSESSMENT OF GOAL

01	02	03	04	05	06	07	08	09	10	11	12	13	14	15	16	17	18	19	20	21	22	23	24	25	26
27	28	29	30	31	32	33	34	35	36	37	38	39	40	41	42	43	44	45	46	47	48	49	50	51	52

GOAL

_____

_____

_____

_____

_____

OBJECTIVES

_____

_____

_____

_____

_____

_____

_____

_____

_____

WEEKLY ASSESSMENT OF GOAL

01	02	03	04	05	06	07	08	09	10	11	12	13	14	15	16	17	18	19	20	21	22	23	24	25	26
27	28	29	30	31	32	33	34	35	36	37	38	39	40	41	42	43	44	45	46	47	48	49	50	51	52

GOAL

_____

_____

_____

_____

_____

OBJECTIVES

_____

_____

_____

_____

_____

_____

_____

_____

_____

_____

WEEKLY ASSESSMENT OF GOAL

01	02	03	04	05	06	07	08	09	10	11	12	13	14	15	16	17	18	19	20	21	22	23	24	25	26
27	28	29	30	31	32	33	34	35	36	37	38	39	40	41	42	43	44	45	46	47	48	49	50	51	52

MONTH

WEEK 1 AND 2

I AM GRATEFUL FOR...

PRIORITIES THIS MONTH

WEEK 3, 4 AND 5

I AM INTELLIGENT
LESSONS I LEARNED THIS MONTH

WINS THIS MONTH

CHALLENGES AND HOW I OVERCAME THEM

WEEK OF _____

TIME	URGENT	SUNDAY	MONDAY	TUESDAY
6am				
7am				
8am				
9am				
10am				
11am				
12pm				
1pm				
2pm				
3pm				
4pm				
5pm				
6pm				
7pm				
8pm				
9pm				
10pm				
DUE				

WEEK OF _____

TIME	WEDNESDAY	THURSDAY	FRIDAY	SATURDAY
6am				
7am				
8am				
9am				
10am				
11am				
12pm				
1pm				
2pm				
3pm				
4pm				
5pm				
6pm				
7pm				
8pm				
9pm				
10pm				
DUE				

WEEK OF _____

TIME	URGENT	SUNDAY	MONDAY	TUESDAY
6am				
7am				
8am				
9am				
10am				
11am				
12pm				
1pm				
2pm				
3pm				
4pm				
5pm				
6pm				
7pm				
8pm				
9pm				
10pm				
DUE				

WEEK OF _____

TIME	WEDNESDAY	THURSDAY	FRIDAY	SATURDAY
6am				
7am				
8am				
9am				
10am				
11am				
12pm				
1pm				
2pm				
3pm				
4pm				
5pm				
6pm				
7pm				
8pm				
9pm				
10pm				
DUE				

WEEK OF _____

TIME	URGENT	SUNDAY	MONDAY	TUESDAY
6am				
7am				
8am				
9am				
10am				
11am				
12pm				
1pm				
2pm				
3pm				
4pm				
5pm				
6pm				
7pm				
8pm				
9pm				
10pm				
DUE				

WEEK OF _____

TIME	WEDNESDAY	THURSDAY	FRIDAY	SATURDAY
6am				
7am				
8am				
9am				
10am				
11am				
12pm				
1pm				
2pm				
3pm				
4pm				
5pm				
6pm				
7pm				
8pm				
9pm				
10pm				
DUE				

WEEK OF _____

TIME	URGENT	SUNDAY	MONDAY	TUESDAY
6am				
7am				
8am				
9am				
10am				
11am				
12pm				
1pm				
2pm				
3pm				
4pm				
5pm				
6pm				
7pm				
8pm				
9pm				
10pm				
DUE				

WEEK OF _____

TIME	WEDNESDAY	THURSDAY	FRIDAY	SATURDAY
6am				
7am				
8am				
9am				
10am				
11am				
12pm				
1pm				
2pm				
3pm				
4pm				
5pm				
6pm				
7pm				
8pm				
9pm				
10pm				
DUE				

WEEKLY REFLECTIONS

WHAT AM I LOOKING FORWARD TO?

THIS WEEKS AFFIRMATION

GOODS THINGS

GOODS DEEDS

WORDS FOR THE WEEK

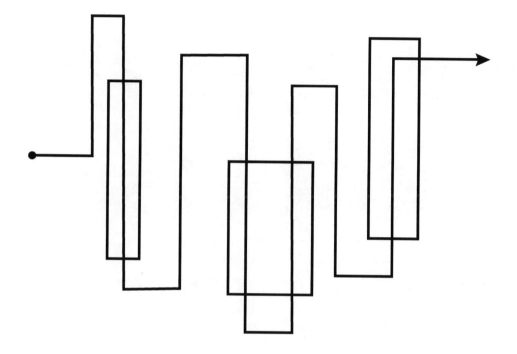

MONTH 1

MONTH

WEEK 1 AND 2

I AM GRATEFUL FOR...

PRIORITIES THIS MONTH

WEEK 3, 4 AND 5

I AM _____

LESSONS I LEARNED THIS MONTH

WINS THIS MONTH

CHALLENGES AND HOW I OVERCAME THEM

W E E K O F _____

TIME	URGENT	SUNDAY	MONDAY	TUESDAY
6am				
7am				
8am				
9am				
10am				
11am				
12pm				
1pm				
2pm				
3pm				
4pm				
5pm				
6pm				
7pm				
8pm				
9pm				
10pm				
DUE				

WEEK OF _____

TIME	WEDNESDAY	THURSDAY	FRIDAY	SATURDAY
6am				
7am				
8am				
9am				
10am				
11am				
12pm				
1pm				
2pm				
3pm				
4pm				
5pm				
6pm				
7pm				
8pm				
9pm				
10pm				
DUE				

WEEK OF _____

TIME	URGENT	SUNDAY	MONDAY	TUESDAY
6am				
7am				
8am				
9am				
10am				
11am				
12pm				
1pm				
2pm				
3pm				
4pm				
5pm				
6pm				
7pm				
8pm				
9pm				
10pm				
DUE				

WEEK OF _____

TIME	WEDNESDAY	THURSDAY	FRIDAY	SATURDAY
6am				
7am				
8am				
9am				
10am				
11am				
12pm				
1pm				
2pm				
3pm				
4pm				
5pm				
6pm				
7pm				
8pm				
9pm				
10pm				
DUE				

WEEK OF _____

TIME	URGENT	SUNDAY	MONDAY	TUESDAY
6am				
7am				
8am				
9am				
10am				
11am				
12pm				
1pm				
2pm				
3pm				
4pm				
5pm				
6pm				
7pm				
8pm				
9pm				
10pm				
DUE				

WEEK OF _____

TIME	WEDNESDAY	THURSDAY	FRIDAY	SATURDAY
6am				
7am				
8am				
9am				
10am				
11am				
12pm				
1pm				
2pm				
3pm				
4pm				
5pm				
6pm				
7pm				
8pm				
9pm				
10pm				
DUE				

WEEK OF _____

TIME	URGENT	SUNDAY	MONDAY	TUESDAY
6am				
7am				
8am				
9am				
10am				
11am				
12pm				
1pm				
2pm				
3pm				
4pm				
5pm				
6pm				
7pm				
8pm				
9pm				
10pm				
DUE				

WEEK OF _____

TIME	WEDNESDAY	THURSDAY	FRIDAY	SATURDAY
6am				
7am				
8am				
9am				
10am				
11am				
12pm				
1pm				
2pm				
3pm				
4pm				
5pm				
6pm				
7pm				
8pm				
9pm				
10pm				
DUE				

WEEKLY REFLECTIONS

WHAT AM I LOOKING FORWARD TO?

THIS WEEKS AFFIRMATION

GOODS THINGS

GOODS DEEDS

WORDS FOR THE WEEK

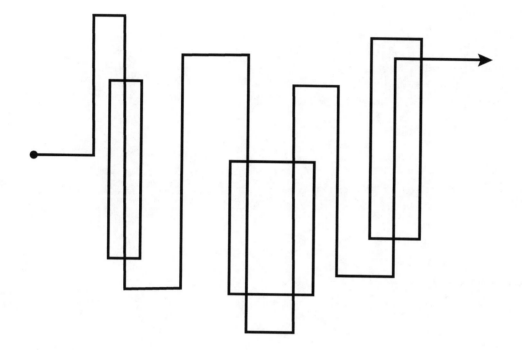

MONTH 2

MONTH _____

WEEK 1 AND 2

I AM GRATEFUL FOR...

PRIORITIES THIS MONTH

WEEK 3, 4 AND 5

I AM _____
LESSONS I LEARNED THIS MONTH

WINS THIS MONTH

CHALLENGES AND HOW I OVERCAME THEM

WEEK OF _____

TIME	URGENT	SUNDAY	MONDAY	TUESDAY
6am				
7am				
8am				
9am				
10am				
11am				
12pm				
1pm				
2pm				
3pm				
4pm				
5pm				
6pm				
7pm				
8pm				
9pm				
10pm				
DUE				

WEEK OF _____

TIME	WEDNESDAY	THURSDAY	FRIDAY	SATURDAY
6am				
7am				
8am				
9am				
10am				
11am				
12pm				
1pm				
2pm				
3pm				
4pm				
5pm				
6pm				
7pm				
8pm				
9pm				
10pm				
DUE				

WEEK OF _____

TIME	URGENT	SUNDAY	MONDAY	TUESDAY
6am				
7am				
8am				
9am				
10am				
11am				
12pm				
1pm				
2pm				
3pm				
4pm				
5pm				
6pm				
7pm				
8pm				
9pm				
10pm				
DUE				

WEEK OF _____

TIME	WEDNESDAY	THURSDAY	FRIDAY	SATURDAY
6am				
7am				
8am				
9am				
10am				
11am				
12pm				
1pm				
2pm				
3pm				
4pm				
5pm				
6pm				
7pm				
8pm				
9pm				
10pm				
DUE				

WEEK OF _____

TIME	URGENT	SUNDAY	MONDAY	TUESDAY
6am				
7am				
8am				
9am				
10am				
11am				
12pm				
1pm				
2pm				
3pm				
4pm				
5pm				
6pm				
7pm				
8pm				
9pm				
10pm				
DUE				

WEEK OF _____

TIME	WEDNESDAY	THURSDAY	FRIDAY	SATURDAY
6am				
7am				
8am				
9am				
10am				
11am				
12pm				
1pm				
2pm				
3pm				
4pm				
5pm				
6pm				
7pm				
8pm				
9pm				
10pm				
DUE				

WEEK OF _____

TIME	URGENT	SUNDAY	MONDAY	TUESDAY
6am				
7am				
8am				
9am				
10am				
11am				
12pm				
1pm				
2pm				
3pm				
4pm				
5pm				
6pm				
7pm				
8pm				
9pm				
10pm				
DUE				

WEEK OF _____

TIME	WEDNESDAY	THURSDAY	FRIDAY	SATURDAY
6am				
7am				
8am				
9am				
10am				
11am				
12pm				
1pm				
2pm				
3pm				
4pm				
5pm				
6pm				
7pm				
8pm				
9pm				
10pm				
DUE				

WEEKLY REFLECTIONS

WHAT AM I LOOKING FORWARD TO?

THIS WEEKS AFFIRMATION

GOODS THINGS

GOODS DEEDS

WORDS FOR THE WEEK

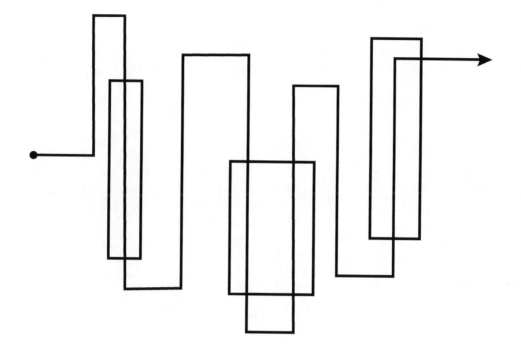

MONTH 3

MONTH _____

WEEK 1 AND 2

I AM GRATEFUL FOR...

PRIORITIES THIS MONTH

WEEK 3, 4 AND 5

I AM _____
LESSONS I LEARNED THIS MONTH

WINS THIS MONTH

CHALLENGES AND HOW I OVERCAME THEM

WEEK OF _____

TIME	URGENT	SUNDAY	MONDAY	TUESDAY
6am				
7am				
8am				
9am				
10am				
11am				
12pm				
1pm				
2pm				
3pm				
4pm				
5pm				
6pm				
7pm				
8pm				
9pm				
10pm				
DUE				

WEEK OF _____

TIME	WEDNESDAY	THURSDAY	FRIDAY	SATURDAY
6am				
7am				
8am				
9am				
10am				
11am				
12pm				
1pm				
2pm				
3pm				
4pm				
5pm				
6pm				
7pm				
8pm				
9pm				
10pm				
DUE				

WEEK OF _____

TIME	URGENT	SUNDAY	MONDAY	TUESDAY
6am				
7am				
8am				
9am				
10am				
11am				
12pm				
1pm				
2pm				
3pm				
4pm				
5pm				
6pm				
7pm				
8pm				
9pm				
10pm				
DUE				

WEEK OF _____

TIME	WEDNESDAY	THURSDAY	FRIDAY	SATURDAY
6am				
7am				
8am				
9am				
10am				
11am				
12pm				
1pm				
2pm				
3pm				
4pm				
5pm				
6pm				
7pm				
8pm				
9pm				
10pm				
DUE				

WEEK OF _____

TIME	URGENT	SUNDAY	MONDAY	TUESDAY
6am				
7am				
8am				
9am				
10am				
11am				
12pm				
1pm				
2pm				
3pm				
4pm				
5pm				
6pm				
7pm				
8pm				
9pm				
10pm				
DUE				

WEEK OF _____

TIME	WEDNESDAY	THURSDAY	FRIDAY	SATURDAY
6am				
7am				
8am				
9am				
10am				
11am				
12pm				
1pm				
2pm				
3pm				
4pm				
5pm				
6pm				
7pm				
8pm				
9pm				
10pm				
DUE				

WEEK OF _____

TIME	URGENT	SUNDAY	MONDAY	TUESDAY
6am				
7am				
8am				
9am				
10am				
11am				
12pm				
1pm				
2pm				
3pm				
4pm				
5pm				
6pm				
7pm				
8pm				
9pm				
10pm				
DUE				

WEEK OF _____

TIME	WEDNESDAY	THURSDAY	FRIDAY	SATURDAY
6am				
7am				
8am				
9am				
10am				
11am				
12pm				
1pm				
2pm				
3pm				
4pm				
5pm				
6pm				
7pm				
8pm				
9pm				
10pm				
DUE				

WEEKLY REFLECTIONS

WHAT AM I LOOKING FORWARD TO?

THIS WEEKS AFFIRMATION

GOODS THINGS

GOODS DEEDS

WORDS FOR THE WEEK

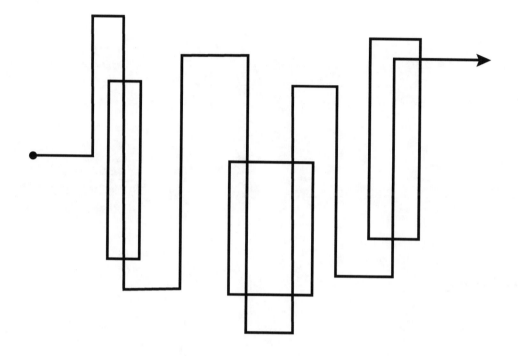

MONTH 4

MONTH

WEEK 1 AND 2

I AM GRATEFUL FOR...

PRIORITIES THIS MONTH

WEEK 3, 4 AND 5

I AM _____
LESSONS I LEARNED THIS MONTH

WINS THIS MONTH

CHALLENGES AND HOW I OVERCAME THEM

WEEK OF _____

TIME	URGENT	SUNDAY	MONDAY	TUESDAY
6am				
7am				
8am				
9am				
10am				
11am				
12pm				
1pm				
2pm				
3pm				
4pm				
5pm				
6pm				
7pm				
8pm				
9pm				
10pm				
DUE				

WEEK OF _____

TIME	WEDNESDAY	THURSDAY	FRIDAY	SATURDAY
6am				
7am				
8am				
9am				
10am				
11am				
12pm				
1pm				
2pm				
3pm				
4pm				
5pm				
6pm				
7pm				
8pm				
9pm				
10pm				
DUE				

WEEK OF _____

TIME	URGENT	SUNDAY	MONDAY	TUESDAY
6am				
7am				
8am				
9am				
10am				
11am				
12pm				
1pm				
2pm				
3pm				
4pm				
5pm				
6pm				
7pm				
8pm				
9pm				
10pm				
DUE				

WEEK OF _____

TIME	WEDNESDAY	THURSDAY	FRIDAY	SATURDAY
6am				
7am				
8am				
9am				
10am				
11am				
12pm				
1pm				
2pm				
3pm				
4pm				
5pm				
6pm				
7pm				
8pm				
9pm				
10pm				
DUE				

WEEK OF _____

TIME	URGENT	SUNDAY	MONDAY	TUESDAY
6am				
7am				
8am				
9am				
10am				
11am				
12pm				
1pm				
2pm				
3pm				
4pm				
5pm				
6pm				
7pm				
8pm				
9pm				
10pm				
DUE				

WEEK OF _____

TIME	WEDNESDAY	THURSDAY	FRIDAY	SATURDAY
6am				
7am				
8am				
9am				
10am				
11am				
12pm				
1pm				
2pm				
3pm				
4pm				
5pm				
6pm				
7pm				
8pm				
9pm				
10pm				
DUE				

WEEK OF _____

TIME	URGENT	SUNDAY	MONDAY	TUESDAY
6am				
7am				
8am				
9am				
10am				
11am				
12pm				
1pm				
2pm				
3pm				
4pm				
5pm				
6pm				
7pm				
8pm				
9pm				
10pm				
DUE				

WEEK OF _____

TIME	WEDNESDAY	THURSDAY	FRIDAY	SATURDAY
6am				
7am				
8am				
9am				
10am				
11am				
12pm				
1pm				
2pm				
3pm				
4pm				
5pm				
6pm				
7pm				
8pm				
9pm				
10pm				
DUE				

WEEKLY REFLECTIONS

WHAT AM I LOOKING FORWARD TO?

THIS WEEKS AFFIRMATION

GOODS THINGS

GOODS DEEDS

WORDS FOR THE WEEK

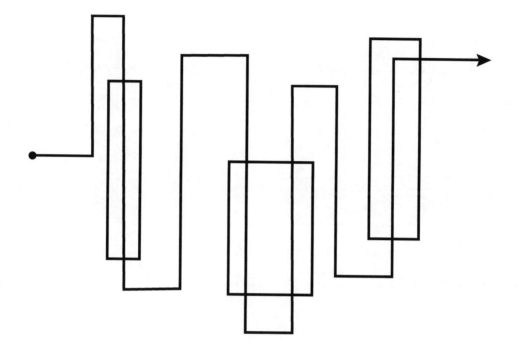

MONTH 5

20 ___ SCHOOL YEAR
COMPLETE WITH SCHOOL HOLIDAYS, EXAMS AND EVENTS.

	SUNDAY	MONDAY	TUESDAY	WEDNESDAY	THURSDAY	FRIDAY	SATURDAY
JULY							
JULY							
JULY							
JULY							
AUGUST							
AUGUST							
AUGUST							
AUGUST							
SEPTEMBER							
SEPTEMBER							
SEPTEMBER							
SEPTEMBER							
OCTOBER							
OCTOBER							
OCTOBER							
OCTOBER							
NOVEMBER							
NOVEMBER							
NOVEMBER							
NOVEMBER							
DECEMBER							
DECEMBER							
DECEMBER							
DECEMBER							

	SUNDAY	MONDAY	TUESDAY	WEDNESDAY	THURSDAY	FRIDAY	SATURDAY
JANUARY							
FEBRUARY							
MARCH							
APRIL							
MAY							
JUNE							

MY SCHEDULE

COMPLETE WITH SCHOOL HOLIDAYS, EXAMS AND EVENTS.

MY SCHEDULE

COMPLETE WITH SCHOOL HOLIDAYS, EXAMS AND EVENTS.

MY SCHEDULE

COMPLETE WITH SCHOOL HOLIDAYS, EXAMS AND EVENTS.

MY SCHEDULE

COMPLETE WITH SCHOOL HOLIDAYS, EXAMS AND EVENTS.

MY SCHEDULE

COMPLETE WITH SCHOOL HOLIDAYS, EXAMS AND EVENTS.

MY SCHEDULE

COMPLETE WITH SCHOOL HOLIDAYS, EXAMS AND EVENTS.

MY SCHEDULE

COMPLETE WITH SCHOOL HOLIDAYS, EXAMS AND EVENTS.

MY SCHEDULE

COMPLETE WITH SCHOOL HOLIDAYS, EXAMS AND EVENTS.

GOALS

A goal is your call to action, it is
what I am going to do and how
am I going to do it. By being
clear about what you want
and how you are going to get
it you write a goal, your dream
becomes a reality and you create
your motivation to achieve
your goals. Here you will write
your S.M.A.R.T. GOALS. Create
academic, extracurricular and
 personal goals.

GOAL

_____

_____

_____

_____

_____

_____

OBJECTIVES

Objectives are the steps to
achieve your goals. Creating
accountability and responsibility
for creating your pathway to
success. An objective may be, To
do all the homework and turn it
 in on time.

OBJECTIVE/ DEFINITION

_____

_____

_____

_____

_____

_____

WEEKLY ASSESSMENT

We were going to put in how to use it. Here check off each week that you have read your
goal and you are working at achieving it. Or celebrate that you have achieved it.

WEEKLY ASSESSMENT OF GOAL

01	02	03	04	05	06	07	08	09	10	11	12	13	14	15	16	17	18	19	20	21	22	23	24	25	26
27	28	29	30	31	32	33	34	35	36	37	38	39	40	41	42	43	44	45	46	47	48	49	50	51	52

GOAL

_____

_____

_____

_____

_____

_____

OBJECTIVES

_____

_____

_____

_____

_____

_____

_____

_____

_____

_____

_____

WEEKLY ASSESSMENT OF GOAL

01	02	03	04	05	06	07	08	09	10	11	12	13	14	15	16	17	18	19	20	21	22	23	24	25	26
27	28	29	30	31	32	33	34	35	36	37	38	39	40	41	42	43	44	45	46	47	48	49	50	51	52

GOAL

_____

_____

_____

_____

_____

OBJECTIVES

_____

_____

_____

_____

_____

_____

_____

_____

_____

WEEKLY ASSESSMENT OF GOAL

01	02	03	04	05	06	07	08	09	10	11	12	13	14	15	16	17	18	19	20	21	22	23	24	25	26
27	28	29	30	31	32	33	34	35	36	37	38	39	40	41	42	43	44	45	46	47	48	49	50	51	52

GOAL

_____

_____

_____

_____

_____

OBJECTIVES

_____

_____

_____

_____

_____

_____

_____

_____

_____

WEEKLY ASSESSMENT OF GOAL

01	02	03	04	05	06	07	08	09	10	11	12	13	14	15	16	17	18	19	20	21	22	23	24	25	26
27	28	29	30	31	32	33	34	35	36	37	38	39	40	41	42	43	44	45	46	47	48	49	50	51	52

GOAL

_____

_____

_____

_____

_____

OBJECTIVES

_____

_____

_____

_____

_____

_____

_____

_____

_____

WEEKLY ASSESSMENT OF GOAL

01	02	03	04	05	06	07	08	09	10	11	12	13	14	15	16	17	18	19	20	21	22	23	24	25	26
27	28	29	30	31	32	33	34	35	36	37	38	39	40	41	42	43	44	45	46	47	48	49	50	51	52

GOAL

OBJECTIVES

WEEKLY ASSESSMENT OF GOAL

01	02	03	04	05	06	07	08	09	10	11	12	13	14	15	16	17	18	19	20	21	22	23	24	25	26
27	28	29	30	31	32	33	34	35	36	37	38	39	40	41	42	43	44	45	46	47	48	49	50	51	52

MONTH

WEEK 1 AND 2

I AM GRATEFUL FOR...

PRIORITIES THIS MONTH

WEEK 3, 4 AND 5

I AM _____

LESSONS I LEARNED THIS MONTH

WINS THIS MONTH

CHALLENGES AND HOW I OVERCAME THEM

WEEK OF _____

TIME	URGENT	SUNDAY	MONDAY	TUESDAY
6am				
7am				
8am				
9am				
10am				
11am				
12pm				
1pm				
2pm				
3pm				
4pm				
5pm				
6pm				
7pm				
8pm				
9pm				
10pm				
DUE				

WEEK OF _____

TIME	WEDNESDAY	THURSDAY	FRIDAY	SATURDAY
6am				
7am				
8am				
9am				
10am				
11am				
12pm				
1pm				
2pm				
3pm				
4pm				
5pm				
6pm				
7pm				
8pm				
9pm				
10pm				
DUE				

WEEK OF _____

TIME	URGENT	SUNDAY	MONDAY	TUESDAY
6am				
7am				
8am				
9am				
10am				
11am				
12pm				
1pm				
2pm				
3pm				
4pm				
5pm				
6pm				
7pm				
8pm				
9pm				
10pm				
DUE				

WEEK OF _____

TIME	WEDNESDAY	THURSDAY	FRIDAY	SATURDAY
6am				
7am				
8am				
9am				
10am				
11am				
12pm				
1pm				
2pm				
3pm				
4pm				
5pm				
6pm				
7pm				
8pm				
9pm				
10pm				
DUE				

WEEK OF

TIME	URGENT	SUNDAY	MONDAY	TUESDAY
6am				
7am				
8am				
9am				
10am				
11am				
12pm				
1pm				
2pm				
3pm				
4pm				
5pm				
6pm				
7pm				
8pm				
9pm				
10pm				
DUE				

WEEK OF _____

TIME	WEDNESDAY	THURSDAY	FRIDAY	SATURDAY
6am				
7am				
8am				
9am				
10am				
11am				
12pm				
1pm				
2pm				
3pm				
4pm				
5pm				
6pm				
7pm				
8pm				
9pm				
10pm				
DUE				

WEEK OF _____

TIME	URGENT	SUNDAY	MONDAY	TUESDAY
6am				
7am				
8am				
9am				
10am				
11am				
12pm				
1pm				
2pm				
3pm				
4pm				
5pm				
6pm				
7pm				
8pm				
9pm				
10pm				
DUE				

WEEK OF _____

TIME	WEDNESDAY	THURSDAY	FRIDAY	SATURDAY
6am				
7am				
8am				
9am				
10am				
11am				
12pm				
1pm				
2pm				
3pm				
4pm				
5pm				
6pm				
7pm				
8pm				
9pm				
10pm				
DUE				

WEEKLY REFLECTIONS

WHAT AM I LOOKING FORWARD TO?

THIS WEEKS AFFIRMATION

GOODS THINGS

GOODS DEEDS

WORDS FOR THE WEEK

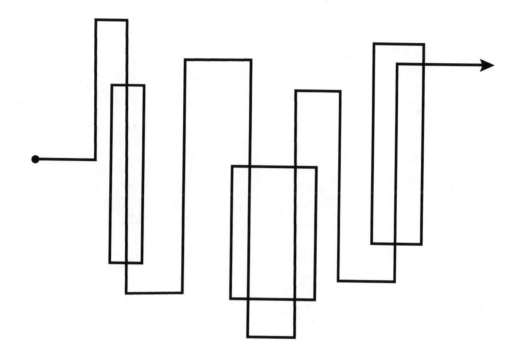

MONTH 6

MONTH

WEEK 1 AND 2

I AM GRATEFUL FOR...

PRIORITIES THIS MONTH

WEEK 3, 4 AND 5

I AM _____
LESSONS I LEARNED THIS MONTH

WINS THIS MONTH

CHALLENGES AND HOW I OVERCAME THEM

WEEK OF _____

TIME	URGENT	SUNDAY	MONDAY	TUESDAY
6am				
7am				
8am				
9am				
10am				
11am				
12pm				
1pm				
2pm				
3pm				
4pm				
5pm				
6pm				
7pm				
8pm				
9pm				
10pm				
DUE				

WEEK OF

TIME	WEDNESDAY	THURSDAY	FRIDAY	SATURDAY
6am				
7am				
8am				
9am				
10am				
11am				
12pm				
1pm				
2pm				
3pm				
4pm				
5pm				
6pm				
7pm				
8pm				
9pm				
10pm				
DUE				

WEEK OF _____

TIME	URGENT	SUNDAY	MONDAY	TUESDAY
6am				
7am				
8am				
9am				
10am				
11am				
12pm				
1pm				
2pm				
3pm				
4pm				
5pm				
6pm				
7pm				
8pm				
9pm				
10pm				
DUE				

WEEK OF _____

TIME	WEDNESDAY	THURSDAY	FRIDAY	SATURDAY
6am				
7am				
8am				
9am				
10am				
11am				
12pm				
1pm				
2pm				
3pm				
4pm				
5pm				
6pm				
7pm				
8pm				
9pm				
10pm				
DUE				

WEEK OF _____

TIME	URGENT	SUNDAY	MONDAY	TUESDAY
6am				
7am				
8am				
9am				
10am				
11am				
12pm				
1pm				
2pm				
3pm				
4pm				
5pm				
6pm				
7pm				
8pm				
9pm				
10pm				
DUE				

WEEK OF _____

TIME	WEDNESDAY	THURSDAY	FRIDAY	SATURDAY
6am				
7am				
8am				
9am				
10am				
11am				
12pm				
1pm				
2pm				
3pm				
4pm				
5pm				
6pm				
7pm				
8pm				
9pm				
10pm				
DUE				

WEEK OF _____

TIME	URGENT	SUNDAY	MONDAY	TUESDAY
6am				
7am				
8am				
9am				
10am				
11am				
12pm				
1pm				
2pm				
3pm				
4pm				
5pm				
6pm				
7pm				
8pm				
9pm				
10pm				
DUE				

WEEK OF _____

TIME	WEDNESDAY	THURSDAY	FRIDAY	SATURDAY
6am				
7am				
8am				
9am				
10am				
11am				
12pm				
1pm				
2pm				
3pm				
4pm				
5pm				
6pm				
7pm				
8pm				
9pm				
10pm				
DUE				

WEEKLY REFLECTIONS

WHAT AM I LOOKING FORWARD TO?

THIS WEEKS AFFIRMATION

GOODS THINGS

GOODS DEEDS

WORDS FOR THE WEEK

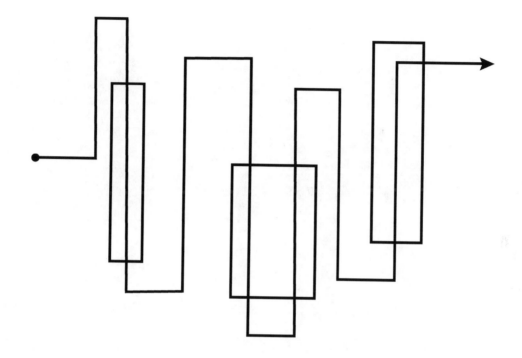

MONTH 7

MONTH

WEEK 1 AND 2

I AM GRATEFUL FOR...

PRIORITIES THIS MONTH

WEEK 3, 4 AND 5

I AM _____

LESSONS I LEARNED THIS MONTH

WINS THIS MONTH

CHALLENGES AND HOW I OVERCAME THEM

WEEK OF _____

TIME	URGENT	SUNDAY	MONDAY	TUESDAY
6am				
7am				
8am				
9am				
10am				
11am				
12pm				
1pm				
2pm				
3pm				
4pm				
5pm				
6pm				
7pm				
8pm				
9pm				
10pm				
DUE				

WEEK OF _____

TIME	WEDNESDAY	THURSDAY	FRIDAY	SATURDAY
6am				
7am				
8am				
9am				
10am				
11am				
12pm				
1pm				
2pm				
3pm				
4pm				
5pm				
6pm				
7pm				
8pm				
9pm				
10pm				
DUE				

WEEK OF _____

TIME	URGENT	SUNDAY	MONDAY	TUESDAY
6am				
7am				
8am				
9am				
10am				
11am				
12pm				
1pm				
2pm				
3pm				
4pm				
5pm				
6pm				
7pm				
8pm				
9pm				
10pm				
DUE				

WEEK OF _____

TIME	WEDNESDAY	THURSDAY	FRIDAY	SATURDAY
6am				
7am				
8am				
9am				
10am				
11am				
12pm				
1pm				
2pm				
3pm				
4pm				
5pm				
6pm				
7pm				
8pm				
9pm				
10pm				
DUE				

WEEK OF _____

TIME	URGENT	SUNDAY	MONDAY	TUESDAY
6am				
7am				
8am				
9am				
10am				
11am				
12pm				
1pm				
2pm				
3pm				
4pm				
5pm				
6pm				
7pm				
8pm				
9pm				
10pm				
DUE				

WEEK OF _____

TIME	WEDNESDAY	THURSDAY	FRIDAY	SATURDAY
6am				
7am				
8am				
9am				
10am				
11am				
12pm				
1pm				
2pm				
3pm				
4pm				
5pm				
6pm				
7pm				
8pm				
9pm				
10pm				
DUE				

WEEK OF _____

TIME	URGENT	SUNDAY	MONDAY	TUESDAY
6am				
7am				
8am				
9am				
10am				
11am				
12pm				
1pm				
2pm				
3pm				
4pm				
5pm				
6pm				
7pm				
8pm				
9pm				
10pm				
DUE				

W E E K   O F _____

TIME	WEDNESDAY	THURSDAY	FRIDAY	SATURDAY
6am				
7am				
8am				
9am				
10am				
11am				
12pm				
1pm				
2pm				
3pm				
4pm				
5pm				
6pm				
7pm				
8pm				
9pm				
10pm				
DUE				

WEEKLY REFLECTIONS

WHAT AM I LOOKING FORWARD TO?

THIS WEEKS AFFIRMATION

GOODS THINGS

GOODS DEEDS

WORDS FOR THE WEEK

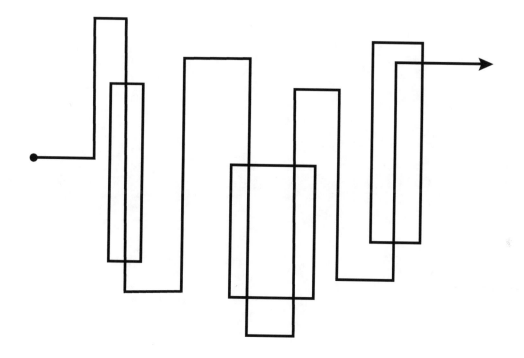

MONTH 8

MONTH

WEEK 1 AND 2

I AM GRATEFUL FOR...

PRIORITIES THIS MONTH

WEEK 3, 4 AND 5

I AM _____
LESSONS I LEARNED THIS MONTH

WINS THIS MONTH

CHALLENGES AND HOW I OVERCAME THEM

WEEK OF _____

TIME	URGENT	SUNDAY	MONDAY	TUESDAY
6am				
7am				
8am				
9am				
10am				
11am				
12pm				
1pm				
2pm				
3pm				
4pm				
5pm				
6pm				
7pm				
8pm				
9pm				
10pm				
DUE				

WEEK OF _____

TIME	WEDNESDAY	THURSDAY	FRIDAY	SATURDAY
6am				
7am				
8am				
9am				
10am				
11am				
12pm				
1pm				
2pm				
3pm				
4pm				
5pm				
6pm				
7pm				
8pm				
9pm				
10pm				
DUE				

WEEK OF _____

TIME	URGENT	SUNDAY	MONDAY	TUESDAY
6am				
7am				
8am				
9am				
10am				
11am				
12pm				
1pm				
2pm				
3pm				
4pm				
5pm				
6pm				
7pm				
8pm				
9pm				
10pm				
DUE				

WEEK OF _____

TIME	WEDNESDAY	THURSDAY	FRIDAY	SATURDAY
6am				
7am				
8am				
9am				
10am				
11am				
12pm				
1pm				
2pm				
3pm				
4pm				
5pm				
6pm				
7pm				
8pm				
9pm				
10pm				
DUE				

WEEK OF

TIME	URGENT	SUNDAY	MONDAY	TUESDAY
6am				
7am				
8am				
9am				
10am				
11am				
12pm				
1pm				
2pm				
3pm				
4pm				
5pm				
6pm				
7pm				
8pm				
9pm				
10pm				
DUE				

WEEK OF _____

TIME	WEDNESDAY	THURSDAY	FRIDAY	SATURDAY
6am				
7am				
8am				
9am				
10am				
11am				
12pm				
1pm				
2pm				
3pm				
4pm				
5pm				
6pm				
7pm				
8pm				
9pm				
10pm				
DUE				

WEEK OF _____

TIME	URGENT	SUNDAY	MONDAY	TUESDAY
6am				
7am				
8am				
9am				
10am				
11am				
12pm				
1pm				
2pm				
3pm				
4pm				
5pm				
6pm				
7pm				
8pm				
9pm				
10pm				
DUE				

WEEK OF _____

TIME	WEDNESDAY	THURSDAY	FRIDAY	SATURDAY
6am				
7am				
8am				
9am				
10am				
11am				
12pm				
1pm				
2pm				
3pm				
4pm				
5pm				
6pm				
7pm				
8pm				
9pm				
10pm				
DUE				

WEEKLY REFLECTIONS

WHAT AM I LOOKING FORWARD TO?

THIS WEEKS AFFIRMATION

GOODS THINGS

GOODS DEEDS

WORDS FOR THE WEEK

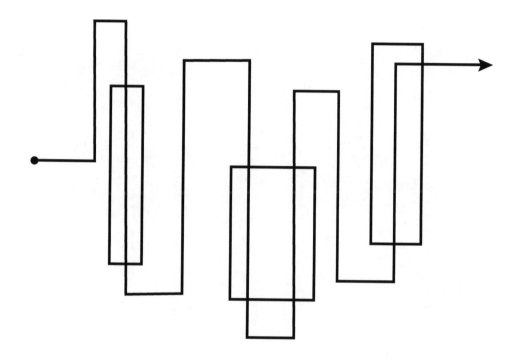

MONTH 9

MONTH

WEEK 1 AND 2

I AM GRATEFUL FOR...

PRIORITIES THIS MONTH

WEEK 3, 4 AND 5

I AM _____
LESSONS I LEARNED THIS MONTH

WINS THIS MONTH

CHALLENGES AND HOW I OVERCAME THEM

WEEK OF _____

TIME	URGENT	SUNDAY	MONDAY	TUESDAY
6am				
7am				
8am				
9am				
10am				
11am				
12pm				
1pm				
2pm				
3pm				
4pm				
5pm				
6pm				
7pm				
8pm				
9pm				
10pm				
DUE				

WEEK OF _____

TIME	WEDNESDAY	THURSDAY	FRIDAY	SATURDAY
6am				
7am				
8am				
9am				
10am				
11am				
12pm				
1pm				
2pm				
3pm				
4pm				
5pm				
6pm				
7pm				
8pm				
9pm				
10pm				
DUE				

WEEK OF _____

TIME	URGENT	SUNDAY	MONDAY	TUESDAY
6am				
7am				
8am				
9am				
10am				
11am				
12pm				
1pm				
2pm				
3pm				
4pm				
5pm				
6pm				
7pm				
8pm				
9pm				
10pm				
DUE				

WEEK OF _____

TIME	WEDNESDAY	THURSDAY	FRIDAY	SATURDAY
6am				
7am				
8am				
9am				
10am				
11am				
12pm				
1pm				
2pm				
3pm				
4pm				
5pm				
6pm				
7pm				
8pm				
9pm				
10pm				
DUE				

WEEK OF _____

TIME	URGENT	SUNDAY	MONDAY	TUESDAY
6am				
7am				
8am				
9am				
10am				
11am				
12pm				
1pm				
2pm				
3pm				
4pm				
5pm				
6pm				
7pm				
8pm				
9pm				
10pm				
DUE				

WEEK OF _____

TIME	WEDNESDAY	THURSDAY	FRIDAY	SATURDAY
6am				
7am				
8am				
9am				
10am				
11am				
12pm				
1pm				
2pm				
3pm				
4pm				
5pm				
6pm				
7pm				
8pm				
9pm				
10pm				
DUE				

WEEK OF _____

TIME	URGENT	SUNDAY	MONDAY	TUESDAY
6am				
7am				
8am				
9am				
10am				
11am				
12pm				
1pm				
2pm				
3pm				
4pm				
5pm				
6pm				
7pm				
8pm				
9pm				
10pm				
DUE				

WEEK OF _____

TIME	WEDNESDAY	THURSDAY	FRIDAY	SATURDAY
6am				
7am				
8am				
9am				
10am				
11am				
12pm				
1pm				
2pm				
3pm				
4pm				
5pm				
6pm				
7pm				
8pm				
9pm				
10pm				
DUE				

WEEKLY REFLECTIONS

WHAT AM I LOOKING FORWARD TO?

THIS WEEKS AFFIRMATION

GOODS THINGS

GOODS DEEDS

WORDS FOR THE WEEK

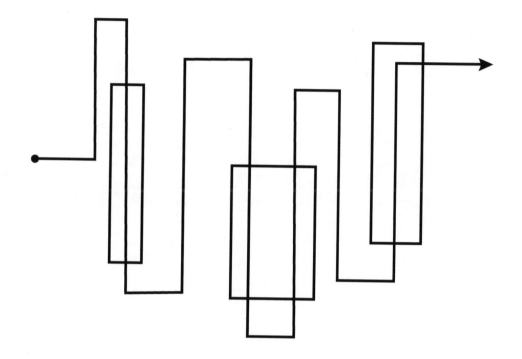

MONTH 10

MONTH

WEEK 1 AND 2

I AM GRATEFUL FOR...

PRIORITIES THIS MONTH

WEEK 3, 4 AND 5

I AM _____
LESSONS I LEARNED THIS MONTH

WINS THIS MONTH

CHALLENGES AND HOW I OVERCAME THEM

WEEK OF _____

TIME	URGENT	SUNDAY	MONDAY	TUESDAY
6am				
7am				
8am				
9am				
10am				
11am				
12pm				
1pm				
2pm				
3pm				
4pm				
5pm				
6pm				
7pm				
8pm				
9pm				
10pm				
DUE				

WEEK OF _____

TIME	WEDNESDAY	THURSDAY	FRIDAY	SATURDAY
6am				
7am				
8am				
9am				
10am				
11am				
12pm				
1pm				
2pm				
3pm				
4pm				
5pm				
6pm				
7pm				
8pm				
9pm				
10pm				
DUE				

WEEK OF _____

TIME	URGENT	SUNDAY	MONDAY	TUESDAY
6am				
7am				
8am				
9am				
10am				
11am				
12pm				
1pm				
2pm				
3pm				
4pm				
5pm				
6pm				
7pm				
8pm				
9pm				
10pm				
DUE				

WEEK OF _____

TIME	WEDNESDAY	THURSDAY	FRIDAY	SATURDAY
6am				
7am				
8am				
9am				
10am				
11am				
12pm				
1pm				
2pm				
3pm				
4pm				
5pm				
6pm				
7pm				
8pm				
9pm				
10pm				
DUE				

WEEK OF _____

TIME	URGENT	SUNDAY	MONDAY	TUESDAY
6am				
7am				
8am				
9am				
10am				
11am				
12pm				
1pm				
2pm				
3pm				
4pm				
5pm				
6pm				
7pm				
8pm				
9pm				
10pm				
DUE				

WEEK OF _____

TIME	WEDNESDAY	THURSDAY	FRIDAY	SATURDAY
6am				
7am				
8am				
9am				
10am				
11am				
12pm				
1pm				
2pm				
3pm				
4pm				
5pm				
6pm				
7pm				
8pm				
9pm				
10pm				
DUE				

W E E K O F _____

TIME	URGENT	SUNDAY	MONDAY	TUESDAY
6am				
7am				
8am				
9am				
10am				
11am				
12pm				
1pm				
2pm				
3pm				
4pm				
5pm				
6pm				
7pm				
8pm				
9pm				
10pm				
DUE				

WEEK OF _____

TIME	WEDNESDAY	THURSDAY	FRIDAY	SATURDAY
6am				
7am				
8am				
9am				
10am				
11am				
12pm				
1pm				
2pm				
3pm				
4pm				
5pm				
6pm				
7pm				
8pm				
9pm				
10pm				
DUE				

WEEKLY REFLECTIONS

WHAT AM I LOOKING FORWARD TO?

THIS WEEKS AFFIRMATION

GOODS THINGS

GOODS DEEDS

WORDS FOR THE WEEK

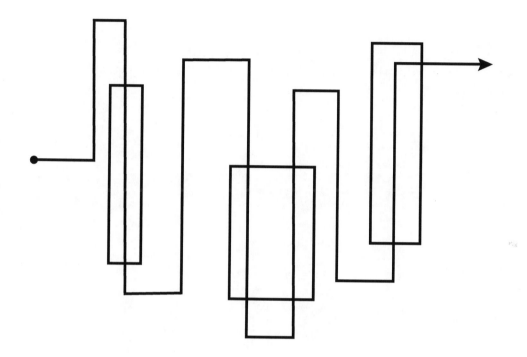

MONTH 11

MONTH

WEEK 1 AND 2

I AM GRATEFUL FOR...

PRIORITIES THIS MONTH

WEEK 3, 4 AND 5

I AM _____
LESSONS I LEARNED THIS MONTH

WINS THIS MONTH

CHALLENGES AND HOW I OVERCAME THEM

WEEK OF _____

TIME	URGENT	SUNDAY	MONDAY	TUESDAY
6am				
7am				
8am				
9am				
10am				
11am				
12pm				
1pm				
2pm				
3pm				
4pm				
5pm				
6pm				
7pm				
8pm				
9pm				
10pm				
DUE				

WEEK OF _____

TIME	WEDNESDAY	THURSDAY	FRIDAY	SATURDAY
6am				
7am				
8am				
9am				
10am				
11am				
12pm				
1pm				
2pm				
3pm				
4pm				
5pm				
6pm				
7pm				
8pm				
9pm				
10pm				
DUE				

WEEK OF _____

TIME	URGENT	SUNDAY	MONDAY	TUESDAY
6am				
7am				
8am				
9am				
10am				
11am				
12pm				
1pm				
2pm				
3pm				
4pm				
5pm				
6pm				
7pm				
8pm				
9pm				
10pm				
DUE				

WEEK OF _____

TIME	WEDNESDAY	THURSDAY	FRIDAY	SATURDAY
6am				
7am				
8am				
9am				
10am				
11am				
12pm				
1pm				
2pm				
3pm				
4pm				
5pm				
6pm				
7pm				
8pm				
9pm				
10pm				
DUE				

WEEK OF _____

TIME	URGENT	SUNDAY	MONDAY	TUESDAY
6am				
7am				
8am				
9am				
10am				
11am				
12pm				
1pm				
2pm				
3pm				
4pm				
5pm				
6pm				
7pm				
8pm				
9pm				
10pm				
DUE				

WEEK OF _____

TIME	WEDNESDAY	THURSDAY	FRIDAY	SATURDAY
6am				
7am				
8am				
9am				
10am				
11am				
12pm				
1pm				
2pm				
3pm				
4pm				
5pm				
6pm				
7pm				
8pm				
9pm				
10pm				
DUE				

WEEK OF _____

TIME	URGENT	SUNDAY	MONDAY	TUESDAY
6am				
7am				
8am				
9am				
10am				
11am				
12pm				
1pm				
2pm				
3pm				
4pm				
5pm				
6pm				
7pm				
8pm				
9pm				
10pm				
DUE				

WEEK OF _____

TIME	WEDNESDAY	THURSDAY	FRIDAY	SATURDAY
6am				
7am				
8am				
9am				
10am				
11am				
12pm				
1pm				
2pm				
3pm				
4pm				
5pm				
6pm				
7pm				
8pm				
9pm				
10pm				
DUE				

WEEKLY REFLECTIONS

WHAT AM I LOOKING FORWARD TO?

THIS WEEKS AFFIRMATION

GOODS THINGS

GOODS DEEDS

WORDS FOR THE WEEK

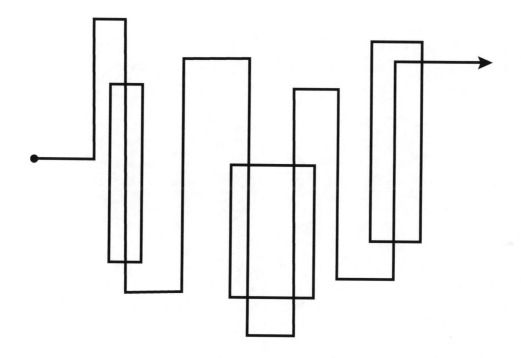

MONTH 12

MONTH

WEEK 1 AND 2

I AM GRATEFUL FOR...

PRIORITIES THIS MONTH

WEEK 3, 4 AND 5

I AM _____
LESSONS I LEARNED THIS MONTH

WINS THIS MONTH

CHALLENGES AND HOW I OVERCAME THEM

WEEK OF _____

TIME	URGENT	SUNDAY	MONDAY	TUESDAY
6am				
7am				
8am				
9am				
10am				
11am				
12pm				
1pm				
2pm				
3pm				
4pm				
5pm				
6pm				
7pm				
8pm				
9pm				
10pm				
DUE				

WEEK OF _____

TIME	WEDNESDAY	THURSDAY	FRIDAY	SATURDAY
6am				
7am				
8am				
9am				
10am				
11am				
12pm				
1pm				
2pm				
3pm				
4pm				
5pm				
6pm				
7pm				
8pm				
9pm				
10pm				
DUE				

WEEK OF _____

TIME	URGENT	SUNDAY	MONDAY	TUESDAY
6am				
7am				
8am				
9am				
10am				
11am				
12pm				
1pm				
2pm				
3pm				
4pm				
5pm				
6pm				
7pm				
8pm				
9pm				
10pm				
DUE				

WEEK OF _____

TIME	WEDNESDAY	THURSDAY	FRIDAY	SATURDAY
6am				
7am				
8am				
9am				
10am				
11am				
12pm				
1pm				
2pm				
3pm				
4pm				
5pm				
6pm				
7pm				
8pm				
9pm				
10pm				
DUE				

WEEK OF _____

TIME	URGENT	SUNDAY	MONDAY	TUESDAY
6am				
7am				
8am				
9am				
10am				
11am				
12pm				
1pm				
2pm				
3pm				
4pm				
5pm				
6pm				
7pm				
8pm				
9pm				
10pm				
DUE				

WEEK OF _____

TIME	WEDNESDAY	THURSDAY	FRIDAY	SATURDAY
6am				
7am				
8am				
9am				
10am				
11am				
12pm				
1pm				
2pm				
3pm				
4pm				
5pm				
6pm				
7pm				
8pm				
9pm				
10pm				
DUE				

WEEK OF _____

TIME	URGENT	SUNDAY	MONDAY	TUESDAY
6am				
7am				
8am				
9am				
10am				
11am				
12pm				
1pm				
2pm				
3pm				
4pm				
5pm				
6pm				
7pm				
8pm				
9pm				
10pm				
DUE				

WEEK OF _____

TIME	WEDNESDAY	THURSDAY	FRIDAY	SATURDAY
6am				
7am				
8am				
9am				
10am				
11am				
12pm				
1pm				
2pm				
3pm				
4pm				
5pm				
6pm				
7pm				
8pm				
9pm				
10pm				
DUE				

WEEKLY REFLECTIONS

WHAT AM I LOOKING FORWARD TO?

THIS WEEKS AFFIRMATION

GOODS THINGS

GOODS DEEDS

WORDS FOR THE WEEK

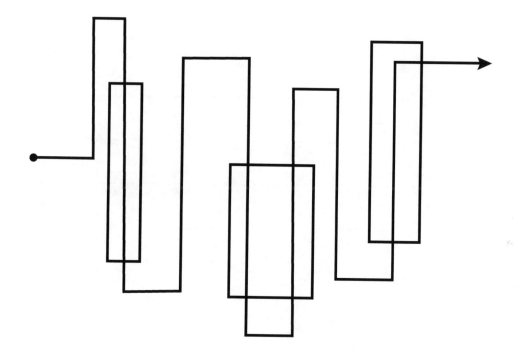

NOTES

NOTES

NOTES

NOTES

NOTES

NOTES